Cryptocurrency 101
2021

Your guide to earning and trading Bitcoin, Altcoin and other currencies online

Table of Contents

.

Introduction

This book is about trading Cryptocurrencies. The premise is that you are new to cryptos. As such, we will take you through a comprehensive introduction to what it is, how it works, and from there you will be able to understand the material on how to trade it.

Cryptocurrencies use a number of terms in the common analog-age lexicon. From the term 'coin' to the term 'blockchains,' to even the concept of 'payment' and 'ownership,' and seemingly unrelated terms like 'mining'. I will tell you here and now, none of these terms are used in the way they used to mean, and you will see why in just a moment.

We will show you what they really mean and put you on the path to understanding how to trade these coins, and what instruments you can use to approach this market with competence and confidence.

We will also show you how to look for opportunities and even use algorithms to trade rapidly, instead of manually clicking the buy or sell button, or manually drawing lines and charts to anticipate movements. We will show you how it works, but we will also explore the software that can do it at lightning speed.

Why would you want to trade Cryptocurrencies?

It's not because it is the latest craze, but because it is the latest money-making potential that rivals the early days of Wall Street, and the Forex market. It is a market that naturally lends itself to electronic trades, and thereby makes entry and exit fluid and efficient. Can you lose money on this? Sure you can. Nothing is guaranteed and, in fact, not only is it not guaranteed, the chances of you losing money trading cryptos is very high if you do not know what you are doing.

That is the perspective we are going to take in this book. We are going to come at it from the perspective of losing money and set up all the necessary tools, strategies, and skills needed to prevent that from happening. That way we have the necessary skills to keep the hard deck.

Once you learn how not to lose money on every trade, you can start to look at the strategies needed to navigate the market and the sentiment. The final step is to get one of two things – either the gut instinct to know a trade in real-time, or to have your AI module trained so well that you can almost fly hands-off.

The central aspect of this book is to get you trading as fast as possible, and to do that you have to get familiar with a load of information, then internalize it so that you can be quick on the draw.

With that in mind, we are going to cover the basics in Chapter One. Once you have an idea of those basics, then we will look at the basics of trading in terms of the where and the how. This is so you will get an idea of how to open an account and what you need to look out for in all the infrastructure to begin trading.

In the third chapter, we will look at the tools you will need. This chapter takes it slow. Here we will look at the basic tools and show you how to hand-fly easy trades.

In the fourth chapter, we will look at conducting day trades and the different statistical indicators that will give you rudimentary buy and sell signals. I will share with you the ones that have brought me success, if used correctly. They need tweaking, and that is part of your growth as a day trader.

In the fifth chapter we will look at automated trading software and how to deploy it. What I am most interested to share with you in the latter part of the chapter is the use of AI in developing auto traders for cryptos. Cryptocurrencies are perfectly suited for this, and you should use the latter part of chapter five as a launch pad for looking at AI as a path toward trading all the various cryptos.

While we are at it, let me just add one basic point about getting a wallet. There are three ways you can do this. You can either get straight to an exchange, pick one and open an account. They will give you the option of keeping all your coins with them online. The second way is by downloading a wallet and keeping your coins in that wallet and moving them to the exchange as and when you need them. Finally, get a small device and load the wallet software on to that, and then transfer what you need to the desktop or laptop that you are trading on as and when you need it.

Let's be clear about wallets. The wallet only does one thing of primary importance (it does other things under the hood too, but they are not important for the trading aspect of cryptos). It keeps the private keys that you have for the address safe and private. In this regard, there are a few things you must understand. It is not only important where you keep your Private Key. It is also important that you don't allow accidental duplication of it. So, for instance, if you are using a wireless system at home, do make sure that you do not transact over that Wi-Fi network because anyone who understands that you are doing this can do what is called a Man in The Middle (MITM) attack, and copy all traffic that is passing through your router. Just keep that in mind.

The next thing is to make sure that you have multiple addresses. A wallet is an app that can hold multiple addresses, and those addresses each have a private key, which you'll need to be able to spend your coin. Create an address for groups of coins and once you have all your coins put into multiple addresses, take what you are not using offline.

When you open your account, it is possible to place all your coins at the exchange. The exchange will keep your coins in a safe wallet, and when you want to withdraw it, you must let them know. In some cases, the withdrawal is instant. In other cases, you may have to wait for a short period. You have to know that keeping your coins in a third-party-controlled wallet is never a good idea, in my opinion. If you can create the necessary measures in your setup, then you will not need to worry about being hacked.

So now that you have an overview of the book, let's dig in and get started.

CHAPTER 1: Fundamentals of Cryptocurrencies

Before we get to trading, let's start with the basics and understand what cryptocurrency is first. Cryptocurrency, or crypto for short, is an electronic form of currency that allows the transmission of value between two nodes on a network. There are two specific networks that you should get familiar with, because they are currently the most widely known and the ones with the most activity. Fair warning: that could change over time. But as long as you understand the basics, it doesn't matter what the branding is. The first network is the Bitcoin network and the second is the Ethereum network.

What do coins and currencies have to do with networks? Think of Bitcoin and Ethereum as two individual networks. Although they comprise of thousands of nodes and hundreds and thousands of users, the ecosystem is a closed loop. The coins never actually leave the network and that network is defined by the existence of nodes.

Nodes

Nodes are computers that are part of the network. To become a node, users download and install the relevant software. The software itself is free, and once installed it opens up a port on the host computer and automatically connects it to a number of other nodes within the network. Each node connects directly to any node in the network, usually only around six at a time. At the last count, there were almost 12,000 of these nodes and each node connects to six others. It may not seem like much, but if you wanted to send a message to the entire network, all you have to do is send it to the six you are connected to and they will relay it to the six each of them is connected to and those nodes will relay that message on, and within 5 to 6 hops, your message will have spread to all 12000 nodes.

Why are messages important? Because the message is the root of the transaction. We will look at the transaction next.

Transaction

The transaction needs to have two elements to it to make it legitimate. First it needs witnesses, and second it needs a reason. A reason is typically, within the Bitcoin network, the movement of tokens from the sender to the receiver. The sender initiates a message on the network messaging system and sends it to the receiver's address.

Imagine if I send you a letter saying that I will give you a dollar and everyone in this town is a witness to that. There is no way of reversing that transaction. The promise is irrevocable. The transaction in Ether or Bitcoin is as simple as that. To initiate a transaction, the sender must have the funds and he must send the message. When he has the funds and sends a message, so that all the nodes bear witness to it, that transaction is legitimized.

Transaction Value

The value of the transaction can be any amount. If it's Bitcoin, it can be as small as 100 millionth of one Bitcoin (0.00000001). That is the smallest value that the messaging system recognizes. It is also called 1 Satoshi (in honor of the person who developed the Bitcoin system). The largest amount is whatever amount you have in that wallet, and you can have as many wallets as you like.

Wallets

Wallets are not the kind that you place in your pocket. On the surface, the wallet is the mailbox that holds the coins that you receive in a message. When you send a message out as part of a transaction, it will come from this mailbox – specifically called an address. If that address (we called it mailbox here for recognition of concept) has previously received coins, then it has the ability to spend those coins. If it has no coins, that address will not be able to send out a transaction message.

A wallet is really an app installed on your device (computer or mobile device) that looks across all the transactions and finds out which transactions in the entire ledger relate to that address. All transactions are categorized as either incoming or outgoing. It adds up all the incoming transactions, and then it separately adds up all the outgoing transactions, and the difference results in your account balance – or the maximum amount that you can transact out.

The only other thing that you need to know is the difference between hot and cold wallets. Hot wallets are ones that are constantly connected to the Internet and accessible at any time. Cold Wallets on the other hand are ones that are not online and can't be accessed via the internet.

The Coin

It's hard to wrap one's mind around the concept of the coin, or the crypto coin as it is also known. The reason is psychological.

We see it as a coin because coins represent tangible currency in our mind. It gives us a frame of reference as a vessel of value. When we mention a coin, it wraps our mind around a new concept using old and familiar vernacular. But the coin in the crypto economy is nothing like the coin we think of that is typically round and flat with engravings on both sides. In fact, all the images you see online that represent Bitcoin as a golden circular coin are merely imaginary. It does not look anything like that.

Some even think of the coin as a string of bits – ones and zeros of binary computer language. But it's not. There is no physical coin, and there is not an electric coin either. In fact the coin is not even cryptographic. I know that this goes against all you have heard, but hang in there, you will see what it is in a minute. What it really is, is a cryptographic intra-network messaging system that cannot be forged or hacked. The key to why it can't be forged or hacked is because it is based on a transparent and decentralized system that is encrypted – more on the encryption and security in the next section.

The coin merely represents an irrevocable act of paying a certain value that is mentioned in the message. And because this is a trustless system, that promise is instantly verified by the system, which knows if the address from where the message is being sent has enough value to be transmitted. It is that value that is described as a coin.

In essence, crypto coin trading is as efficient and pure as it gets, because you are trading our purchasing value. But because it is hard for most people, who are not deeply familiar with the inner workings of the system, the term 'coin' gives them a sense of comfort by referring them to the objectification of the value that is being transmitted.

For the promise to have value, it must have been derived from value. You cannot just take something and arbitrarily bestow value upon it. Before it can have market value or face value, it must first have some form of intrinsic value. Without that the value is untradeable. You must understand this at the core of your foray into crypto-economics and cryptocurrency trading.

The intrinsic value the 'coin' gets is derived from the physical labor that is performed to bring that 'coin' into existence. Resources need to be spent, and effort needs to be applied in creating each 'coin,' and that is why it is referred to as mining. Just as precious metals need to be physically mined, cryptographic value needs to be created by the expense of computational resources and cryptographic processes, and this is done by mining. The next section will describe the mining process.

Essentially, then, coins are brought to life as a reward for the mining process, which requires the expense of resource and cannot be derived for free. It is the nature of the Bitcoin system. In Ethereum, the expense of bringing a coin into existence is done by the expense of resources as well, but they will be converting from the Proof of Work model to the Proof of Stake model in the coming months, barring any unforeseen changes. Either way, a value of some sort needs to be applied.

Once the coin is received by the person who expends this effort, he has the ability to spend it any way he wants. He can even give it away for free or he can use it as consideration for any product or service, as long as the recipient is willing to accept it. But let's look at that carefully for a minute.

The person who receives it from the system is called the miner, and we will explain that next, but for now, just know that in return for his mining, the system gives him and only him a certain number of coins (remember that coins in this context is just a value with no physical features). When he spends that coin, he can only do it within the network. Of course, he can purchase whatever he wants, as long as the person he is buying from is within the network and has a valid address to receive that payment.

So now that value expended during the mining can be exchanged for anything and it is done so by a message that forms the transaction.

When you trade, that is what you are trading. That is what is called a coin.

Mining

Mining is discussed in this book for two reasons. The first is that it gives you an opportunity to invest in Cryptocurrencies in the form of mining. Even though you are interested in trading, mining is a form of investment in cryptos that are worth thinking about because the cost of mining has only a few factor inputs: electricity to run the computers, purchase of the computers, and the software and whatever labor costs the miner needs to perform the tasks. The hardware costs are typically one-off (there are also replacement costs, because the processors can burn out and might need replacing). Once you acquire the coins in this way, you can then use them to trade. That's one way of doing it. But not everyone wants to get knee-deep in the process. For those folks, we advise just getting to the exchange and starting your trading from there.

We mentioned earlier that mining is the process that brings the coins to life. But now we are going to look closely at what that is. In the next section, we will talk about the blockchain and what it is, but for now, just know that it exists.

While mining efforts result in rewards in the form of coins, the actual mining is the process of computation. In other words, mining is just really a ring of millions of computations to solve a puzzle. The first one to solve that puzzle will be awarded the coin. Thus, the question here is: what is the puzzle?

Without going in too deep, the puzzle relates to hashing. Hashing is a branch of mathematical cryptography that uses a one-way function that is deterministic. That means if I took a word and hashed it, I would get an unpredictable sequence of characters that cannot be reverse engineered. I could take this entire book and hash it and what I will get is a string of characters that look like this (this is the hash of the following sentence: The rise and fall of the Roman Empire):

5C94D7845A6A2163D39CA32A0D19122C6B95FA591CF58636DBEBB475EDA4A160

That hash is so unbreakable that even if I were to change one letter, or even the capitalization of that letter, see how the entire hash changes. I will hash the same sentence but with a minor change: the rise and fall of the Roman Empire. In this case, if you notice, the first alphabet has been changed to a lowercase.

AFC44E6D243443A56A2D65357FA98EA61A6A5997BD2975C4435B9A4BCCCFB763

If you observe the two hashes, they look very different. There is no way you could reverse engineer it, even if you knew how it was hashed.

Now remember, these are just the basic parts of hashing. If you want to know more, there are numerous books that you can get to understand the hashing and cryptographic process in deeper detail.

Back to mining.

Every time a transaction is completed (a message to send coin from one account to another is broadcast through the network) two things happen. The first is the nodes that receive the broadcast check to see if it is a valid transaction – specifically they see if the sender has a sufficient balance. The second thing they do is confirm if the message is properly formatted and all the details are present. There are about 16 checks that the nodes execute, and if all is okay, they place the transaction in a queue. At this point the transfer of value is not yet confirmed.

There are hundreds of these messages on an hourly basis in the queue.

The next thing that happens is the miners pull all these transactions (they take the transaction IDs) and put them together and hash them. There is a specific way to hash them and it has to include a few things. It needs to include the TXIDs, the header, the hash of the last block, and one more item called a nonce.

This nonce is a random number, but this is where the puzzle that needs to be solved comes into play. If you take all the information that goes into the block and run the hash function, it will result in a specific string of characters – just as the sentence "The rise and fall of the Roman Empire" above did.

Now look at the sentence again, and the corresponding hash for it:

The rise and fall of the Roman Empire

AFC44E6D243443A56A2D65357FA98EA61A6A5997BD2975C4435B9A4BCCCFB763

The rule is that you can't change any part of the sentence, but you can add random characters after it. With that in mind, what if I told you that the puzzle was to find the hash that started with the character 0 (zero)? Since you can't reverse engineer the hash, you have to randomly keep trying with different strings of characters that you can append to the sentence to make the hash start with 0. It would look something like this:

The rise and fall of the Roman Empire 5134525

52CBF3DF5DFA63DA68F55AA5BC321F36597E53D96001B5D1E14668DE79F444E7

This wouldn't work because the resulting hash didn't begin with 0 as the system required.

The next try:

The rise and fall of the Roman Empire 4749q0r58tj

423C9570BC80747EC346626C8049208DBA52753BA303516817D9CFC6390D1D10

This didn't work either. But just to make the point, after a few hundred tries the random number that worked was this:

The rise and fall of the Roman Empire 090989897934

Which resulted in the hash as below:

0C3EE05D5788E2FD0DFE4D49AE6109A1AFE36523F0D99ED6DC48A4ECF8681622

That hash satisfied the requirement, and as such, the puzzle is solved.

Once the puzzle is solved, the coins are awarded to the miner that solved the puzzle and all the transactions that were included are now said to be part of a block with a specific hash. That hash becomes part of the record and can never be altered. If the block can't be altered (because if you alter the block, the hash would change, and the system would know that there was a problem and reject that block) then the transactions within it can't be altered, either.

Once that block is confirmed, all the transactions in that block are confirmed and the person who received a payment will now see that his payment is confirmed. So, on one side, the mining keeps the integrity of the coins, and on the other side, it generates more coins into the system.

You can't change any of the transaction IDs without changing the hash. This keeps the whole thing secure.

Blockchain

In the last section we talked, in passing, of a Blockchain. Now, it is time to look at that in a little more detail. If you notice that the messages that the sender initiates are not just sent to the address he is sending the coin to, he sends it to all nodes in the network – via the six (or more) nodes he is directly connected to. In just a few seconds that message reverberates across the entire network and all the nodes take note of that message. Once that message is released, and the rest of the nodes bear witness to it, the nodes now deem that the recipient is now the owner of more coins, and that the sender has less.

Let's put this to use in an example.

Let's say Andy wants to pay Bob 1 BTC (BTC = Bitcoin) for whatever reason, which is immaterial to the network. Bob creates a wallet and gets an address. That address belongs to him and it comes with a Private Key. In the meantime, Andy, who already has his address, Private Key, and some Bitcoin in his wallet, takes Bob's address from him and broadcasts a message to the entire network that he is sending Bob 1 BTC. You've already seen how that is then placed in blocks.

Once it is placed in a block, the entire block is hashed, and that is then placed inside the next block and the miner proceeds to solve the puzzle. Once the puzzle is solved, that hash is then placed in the next block of transactions, and so on it goes.

That results in an unbreakable chain. Once the transaction is confirmed, it cannot be canceled or reversed. It lives forever, because a change in even one digit will change the hash, and that change in hash will not jive with the hash that is already recorded in the preceding block.

This blockchain record is kept on all full nodes. That means there are thousands of records of this blockchain, which means it can't be altered.

The fundamentals of Cryptocurrencies in this chapter looked primarily at Bitcoin and to a brief extent, Ethereum. But all cryptos have some form of mechanism that is similar. All of them have the same concept but execute it differently, and by that you get different coins and networks.

The volume of coin demanded and the supply at any given point give rise to a value, and that value is made more fluid and the asset is made more liquid by a vibrant market. Trading in Cryptocurrencies is a three-dimensional proposition. You can either trade fiats for cryptos, or you can trade one crypto for another. We will get into those details in the next chapter.

Buckle up!

CHAPTER 2:

Basics of Trading

Trading cryptos is simple. You buy one of many existing Cryptocurrencies that are offered by the exchanges. There are a number of exchanges that exist in the US and in other parts of the world. Before you think about where you want to open an account, here is what you need to consider.

The first thing is that you need to open an account. If you prefer, you can open an account in a location that is not going to impose a tax liability on you in any jurisdiction. So this deserves some study. This book is not going to give you tax advice, but you should know that there are jurisdictions that will consider profits from Bitcoin trading to be taxable. If you look at it as a currency, and that it is not legal sovereign tender, then it is tempting to think that it is not taxable. This is wrong. Most tax jurisdictions do not differentiate the underlying asset when accounting for profit.

The other thing that people are quick to assume is that Bitcoin transactions are anonymous. Well, they are to a limited extent. But there are easy ways to see who owns what, unless you go through extreme measures to protect it. When people say that Bitcoin is usually used by the shady elements to hide their activities, they don't really know what they are talking about.

Exchanges

There are more than a hundred exchanges that you can get on to be able to trade the currencies that we talk about in this book. We will stick to one hundred, and you can look at each one of them to see which ones you would like to pick. You should have at least 10 exchanges in your basket, and you should use the ones that allow you to keep your coins wherever you please and transfer to them only when your trades are open, find an exchange that is quick with withdrawals and an exchange that executes rapidly without the need for brokers. Brokers work against your interests because they cost more and they are unable to execute rapid trades. Here is a list of exchanges that you can evaluate:

1   Abucoins

2   ACX

3   AEX

4   AidosMarket

5   alcurEX

6   Allcoin

7   Altcoin Trader

8   Bancor Network

9   BarterDEX

10   BCEX

11   Bibox

12	BigONE
13	Binance
14	Bisq
15	Bit-Z
16	Bit2C
17	Bitbank
18	BitBay
19	Bitcoin Indonesia
20	BitcoinToYou
21	BitcoinTrade
22	Bitex
23	Bitfinex
24	BitFlip
25	bitFlyer
26	Bithumb
27	Bitinka
28	BitKonan
29	Bitlish
30	BitMarket
31	Bitmaszyna
32	Bitonic
33	Bits Blockchain
34	Bitsane
35	BitShares Asset Exchange

36	Bitso
37	Bitstamp
38	Bitstamp (Ripple Gateway)
39	Bittrex
40	Bittylicious
41	BL3P
42	Bleutrade
43	Braziliex
44	BTC Markets
45	BTC Trade UA
46	BTC-Alpha
47	BTCC
48	BtcTrade
49	BTCTurk
50	Burst Asset Exchange
51	BX Thailand
52	C-CEX
53	C-Patex
54	C2CX
55	CEX
56	ChaoEX
57	Cobinhood
58	Coinbe
59	Coinbene

60	CoinCorner
61	CoinEgg
62	CoinEx
63	CoinExchange
64	CoinFalcon
65	Coinfloor
66	Coingi
67	Coinhouse
68	Coinlink
69	CoinMate
70	Coinnest
71	Coinone
72	Coinrail
73	Coinrate
74	Coinroom
75	CoinsBank
76	Coinsecure
77	Coinsquare
78	Coinut
79	COSS
80	Counterparty DEX
81	CryptoBridge
82	CryptoDerivatives
83	CryptoMarket

84	Cryptomate
85	Cryptopia
86	Cryptox
87	DC-Ex
88	DDEX
89	Dgtmarket
90	DSX
91	ETHEXIndia
92	ExcambrioRex
93	Exchange
94	Exmo
95	Exrates
96	EXX
97	ezBtc
98	Fargobase
99	Fatbtc
100	Foxbit
101	FreiExchange
102	Gate
103	Gatecoin
104	Gatehub
105	GDAX
106	Gemini
107	GetBTC

108	GuldenTrader
109	Heat Wallet
110	HitBTC
111	Huobi
112	IDAX
113	IDEX
114	Independent Reserve
115	InfinityCoin Exchange
116	Iquant
117	ISX
118	itBit
119	Koineks
120	Koinex
121	Koinim
122	Korbit
123	Kraken
124	Kucoin
125	Kuna
126	LakeBTC
127	Lbank
128	LEOxChange
129	Liqui
130	LiteBit
131	Livecoin

180	Upbit
181	Vebitcoin
182	VirtacoinWorld
183	Waves Decentralized Exchange
184	WEX
185	xBTCe
186	YoBit
187	Zaif
188	ZB
189	Zebpay

** Please note that these sites have not been vetted, and as such you need to do your own due diligence before using their services.

Market

If you want to trade cryptos actively, it is not a difficult process once you get your fundamental study and technical study internalized. There are few, if any, regulations on it that you need to abide by, and as long as you do not engage in fraud or theft, and you conduct yourself equitably, you won't need to keep looking over your shoulder.

Remember that cryptos are not physical assets like shares of companies, or fiat currencies that have the legal sovereign banking system – and then further substantiated by other countries, and by the world's banking institutions. Currencies have that, cryptos don't. So that is the first risk that you need to keep way back in your mind. What's the worst that can happen to cryptos? They could be outlawed around the world. The chance of that happening is low, but nonetheless it exists. In our case, that is a good thing because it adds to the push and pull of the market, creating opportunities to buy and sell. It is also one of the reasons you should not keep an open position overnight.

More importantly, unlike shares and currency, they are not physical assets that can be held and kept – cryptos are not physical in any form. These are conceptual assets, and as we advance as a society we will see that cryptos will end up being the most efficient currency in use. Imagine a time when we eventually reach space and have colonies – cryptos would be an ideal way to facilitate commerce.

Up until this point, what we have been looking at has been the ecosystem of the crypto economy – specifically the cryptocurrency. That gives us the basic knowledge to start understanding the factors that come into play for the market that we are interested in. Our next goal is to look at the market. I will compare the crypto market to traditional financial markets, if necessary.

The first thing you need to know is that the crypto market is not centrally regulated. That means there are no rules yet on what you can and can't do, but there are limitations as to what is acceptable in the marketplace. You can trade manually, you can use program trading, and you can even use artificial intelligence.

There are no rules, and that makes it a very lucrative opportunity if you do three things. The first is make sure you understand the basics. Second, start small – the minimum trading size for a few exchanges is 0.001 BTC. You need to get the feel for how things happen, and that gets your confidence and experience up. The third is that you do not stop at plain vanilla trades. If you just want to get into it and trade one or two times a day with plain vanilla trades, then this is not something that you will succeed at in the way that you imagine. Bottom line: start small and crank it up.

I hear many would-be traders complain that the Bitcoin market is volatile. It is, but that is a good thing. There are two kinds of volatility. One where there is high volume (and the volatility is driven by a different factor) and the other where there is insufficient volume.

Tradability

Bitcoin is not the only crypto out there that you can trade. And the USD is not the only fiat that you can trade that against. There are over 1000 cryptos in the market today and over 100 fiats that are worth trading. However, mastering all those pairings creates a nightmare. You should focus on just a few. In my experience, the US Dollar, the Japanese Yen, and the Euro are your best fiats to be traded against cryptos. Among the cryptos, aside from Bitcoin, which is the obvious trading opportunity, there are eight alternatives you can choose from as follows: Ethereum, Litecoin, NEM, Dash, Ripple, Ethereum Classic, Monero, and Zcash.

That gives you more than 50 possible trading pairs - USD v BTC, USD v ETH, USD v NEM, and so on. It may seem like a wide field to choose from, but let me tell you that, as a beginner, it is indeed too many. As a manual trader, it will be completely overwhelming for you to understand, track, and execute the entry and exits of each pair.

To effectively choose the pairing, you need to be intimately familiar with the nature of the individual currency and the nature of their pairing. To do this you need to observe and understand the critical factors of tradability and liquidity.

Tradability is a combination of volatility and breadth. Volatility is the frequency of movement that it makes in a given period of time, and breadth is about the gap between the movement of the price's high and low. You need both to make it tradable. Tradability is a lot different from buying and holding for future profit. That does not require the higher frequency movements. On the other hand, if there is no breadth, then it will be hard to enter and exit the market profitably, since there are spreads that you need to consider. For instance, if you are looking at a pairing between A and B, the exchange rate is 1:1.9. In actuality, the rate is spread between 1.85 and 1.95. Your buy price would be 1.95 in this example and your sell price would be 1.85. This spread would cause you to lose 0.1 if you were to do an instant entry and exit. The point of highlighting this is to show you that, even if the price didn't move, if you entered and exited within moments, you would still lose the spread.

Because of this, breadth of movement is important, especially if you want to do fast trades, which cryptos are capable of. You want to be able to have it move at least across the spread and cover your fees and other costs, and if that happened, you could scalp the market many times during the day and make a tidy profit. We will look at this again later.

The way volatility helps is that it gives you many opportunities to trade in a day. You need to think about trading as a two-way street, and not as you would if you were buying stocks. In this two-way street, you are exchanging one currency for another. And so, if you think that BTC v ETH is rapidly fluctuating, that means the BTC will rise against ETH and then fall back. When BTC falls back against ETH, it means the ETH is momentarily appreciating. Your opportunity comes from riding those ups and downs.

If an asset is not volatile, it may be a great asset to purchase for the long-term, but it won't be a good candidate to trade rapidly or day trade – which is what you want to do with cryptos. Try not to leave a position overnight when it comes to these assets. It is too high a risk to leave open positions unattended – unless you are doing program trading or using AI.

The crypto market is unlike the stock market. If they are not volatile, they present no opportunity to trade profitability – remember we are talking about trading here. Buying an asset for long-term appreciation is not covered in this discussion.

On the other hand, if they are too volatile, they present reduced security and predictability to trade. So a balance must exist in the level of volatility. These untenable volatile situations arise due to volume. If the volume is low, prices tend to be volatile but they are not tradable. This is because the price fluctuates too rapidly to allow the entry into the market to be predictable, and then once in, it becomes too difficult to exit the market effectively. The average volume is a key factor in accepting the volatility pattern of the asset. This leads us to liquidity – the second of the two factors we mentioned.

<u>What is liquidity?</u>

Liquidity has to do to with volume and efficiency. You can think of it as friction. If you get into an asset, you want it to be as frictionless as possible. That means you get in when you want to and you get out when you want to. There are a few situations that may make that untenable. One scenario that could happen is when everyone wants to sell, you will find that there are no buyers – that's not a liquid market. You may discover that finding a seller or finding a buyer is not easy because there is lackluster interest in the asset; or you may find that there are not enough exchanges supporting the market, which reduces the potential trader's access to that asset. These are just a few ways the asset is illiquid – there are more. But you get the point. When you consider an asset, you need to assess its liquidity and its volatility. Liquidity without volatility does not give you tradability, while volatility without liquidity doesn't give you predictability.

This is partially the reason Bitcoin is more valuable and in demand than its alternatives and the USD-BTC pair is a popular investment tool for day traders. It is also because there is sufficient liquidity to make your trades almost seamless and efficient. This is called a liquidity premium, and it is one that you should be willing to pay, as the payoff is worth it.

But that is a fiat-crypto pair (meaning it is the trade between a fiat currency and a cryptocurrency). What about a crypto-crypto pair? Well, there are several large volume and liquid pairs that you can work with. One such pair is the BTC-ETH pair.

With respect to tradability, you should have your basket well differentiated between fiat-cryptos and crypto-cryptos, and even have a basket that is fiat-crypto-fiat or crypto-fiat-crypto, or some other three-way combination.

You want to be an expert in at least two or three combinations, and that expertise comes in the form of study and practice. You have to study the fundamentals and you have to practice the art of reading the charts. In the trading business these are called the fundamentals and the technical. You have to study the fundamentals – which includes knowledge of the asset, how it works, market sentiment, regulation, and analysis. On the other hand you have to know how to read the charts. The charts and the analysis of the movement of price is a comprehensive mathematical and statistical representation of the psychology of the market. It is fairly plausible to understand where the market is moving in the future by looking at sufficient data from the past. That's the technical aspect of the analysis.

Become an expert at BTC vs Ethereum and BTC vs USD to start.

CHAPTER 3:

Crypto Trading

There are two ways you can get into active trading. One has a cost advantage, so it is good to get started with this. The second has an accuracy and professional advantage but the costs are significantly higher. It's not always a simple choice between one and the other, but rather a case of growing from one and moving on to the next.

When you start off, it is best that you take the one that gives you the cost-benefit, this is assuming that you start slowly. If your initial foray into the market is between 5 and 10 Bitcoin, then going online would not be too obstructive. With that amount, you would probably conduct between three and five trades per day (24 hours). In this case, the online exchanges are absolutely fine.

The online exchanges and trading houses provide you with the ability to execute trades, as well as use trading tools to find buy and sell points. A few of the reputable intermediaries have this, and most of them are free if you place a certain minimum amount with them.

The other option is for you to stay away from the online trading platform and get the price feed you need from the Bloomberg Terminal. Bloomberg now offers real-time quotes for most of the major cryptos, and even some of the more recent ones. It is surprisingly extensive. When I first started using it, they only had the USD-BTC pair and over the last few years they have added most of the others. They also offer the ability to chart all the cryptos and even give you the flexibility to program your strategy directly from your feed. My current setup pulls the real-time feed from the terminal, which then gets fed into an AI algorithm that we have developed.

If you are considering taking this on with any level of seriousness, then you should not skimp on the equipment that you are going to need. If you do decide to go the Bloomberg Terminal route, then go ahead and get the T1 line put in as well. That way you are getting super-fast real-time feeds on pricing.

If you end up doing trades that are rapid-fire, and if you use an online system, even if you do have broadband, then you will end up having a lag time, which is not acceptable for any level of serious trading.

When I got into trading, I had no choice but to do it online, but jumped to BT as soon as they started to offer it. The speed of the T1 line and the accuracy of the prices allows me to execute rapid turnarounds and trade higher volumes in a day and to have higher frequency of multiple pairs. 90% of my trades are not manual, they are program trades, 5% are AI trades, and 5% are manual trades.

When you do program trades, the programs are scanning for opportunities across the market at a rate that is significantly more efficient than a human possibly could. This brings more trading opportunities to my attention, which increases my volume and my profit potential. I suggest you do the same.

Trading Strategies

There are three trading strategies introduced in this chapter. These strategies will form the foundation of other strategies that you will surely get used to as you mature in your trading abilities. This is assuming that you are new to cryptocurrency trading and have minimal knowledge and understanding of what it is and how to do it.

Remember that this market moves constantly. Hardly a second that goes by when a trade is not being conducted. With more than 50 pairs of currencies and fiats, trading can easily become a full-time occupation.

Buy the Dips

Always remember to buy the dips. Dips are moments in the price movement that a march forward is followed by a momentary step back. This is the characteristic of most markets. When you are new to any market, it is an effective way to identify trends. When you are day trading, trends are not what they would be if you were a long-term trader. A long-term trader considers a trend to last anything from a few days to a few months, and enters his position and leaves it for days, weeks, or even months. A scalper in cryptos or a day trader doesn't do that. He actively trades the waves, both up and down, and exits in minutes, or hours, at the most.

Since you are doing rapid trades, you can use the dips to get a better entry point once a mini-rally has started. This is your first strategy. When you first get started, observe the graphical representation of price movements. Don't look at the numbers, as the numbers can't give you an image of the price as it takes shape. Watch the chart and adjust the timescale to 5 seconds, 10 seconds, and 1 minute to get an idea of the nature of the movement. You will notice that every advance is punctuated by a retracement and every fall is retarded by a momentary uptick. Get used to this patter and use it in your ability to buy the dip.

Never place an order as soon as the market turns from one trend to the next. Wait for the dip, then buy on its next run. That way you can see the rally form rather than face the retracements soon as you get in. It also gives you an opportunity to confirm the push forward. Use the dips as a trigger for your market entry.

Do the same thing when you are shorting the market - wait for the dip. In this case, the dip means that it is backing off its downward trend and momentarily ascending. Wait for it. When it reaches its apex and starts back down, that's when you catch it. Make it a habit to never try to catch it at its peak. Fortune may grant a perfect catch while the price peaks, but it's never a good long-term habit to have.

The apex and the pit have a specific purpose, and that purpose is not for you to harvest or liquidate, but for you to prepare for the next move. Those are your trigger points.

Arbitrage

This is an advanced strategy only as far as beginners go, but it is something that you should master right away. Arbitrage doesn't focus on the ups and downs of the market, but rather the mispricing of the market. In cryptos, this is an underutilized strategy, and if nothing else, this is the strategy you should take away from this book.

When there are so many pairings, your best bet is to use the automated programs that I use (as described in the earlier part of this chapter). Without automation, you are not going to be able to make use of the greatest benefit that cryptos provide – and that is tradability and volatility.

Back to arbitrage.

In arbitrage, the thing that you are looking for is a mismatch in price between pairs. So, let's say for instance you have the price of A vs B, price of B vs C, and the price of C vs A. If all goes well, and the A:B is 1:2, B:C is 1:3, then it should be that A:C should be priced at 1:6. But in a pricing mismatch, A (in this example) is bidding at 1:6.5. What happens in this case? Look at how simple this is. If I use one unit of A to buy C, I get 6.5 in return. With 6.5, I can use C to buy B at the rate of 1:3, which will get me 2.167 of B. With 2.167 of B I exchange that back into A to get 1.08 of A. When I first started the arbitrage exercise, I walked in with only 1 unit of A and I exited with 1.08 units of A. This example shows an 8% return. That's not so important, because the numbers are only examples. The point is that this trade would take just 30 seconds to complete.

Now let's look at how you set this up on your trading. Before I forget, there is something that you should do on a daily basis. On any given day, there are numerous mispricing opportunities, and you will not be able to catch all of them manually. You will need a program or an AI algorithm to catch them and execute the trades. Just keep the program running and set it up to either trade automatically, or to seek your approval prior to placing the trade.

If you don't do this, there are a number of other traders who are going to do it. The fastest to execute this gets the prize. The guys who trade on web-based portals are certainly not going to be in the running. Because, to take advantage of this, you need extremely low-latency systems and real-time data feeds. Your Bloomberg Terminal can do it, only if you are on a T1 line.

On Balance Volume

The two strategies you've seen so far are really enough to get you started, but here is a third one that goes beyond just buying and selling when and if you 'feel' like it. The logic behind the first one, on the surface, is designed to get you to identify market entry and market exit triggers. On a deeper level it is designed to get you familiarized with the nature of price movements and the use of charts to visualize them. The second strategy was arbitrage, and that was designed to get you to profit off the mispricing of the market. That's on the surface. From a deeper perspective, it is designed to get you to open your mind to the different ways of taking advantage of the markets.

This last of the three strategies is designed to get you to see what the smart money is doing. By using this strategy, you are keeping an eye on where all the money is flocking to. If you can get comfortable with the movement of big money, then you can pretty much ride the trends and scalp the fluctuations.

To do this you need an OBV indicator. Bloomberg has it preinstalled on the Terminal. Some prominent MT4 for cryptos have it as well. OBV stands for On Balance Volume.

The OBV indicator gives you insight into how much money is flowing into any given position. What happens when you see money pouring into a currency? You know that it is about to take off. One of the things that you don't normally see in the online or web-based trading platforms is the volume of orders that are going in the pipeline. When you watch that with the OBV, what you get is pretty good insight into where the market is going to tip at any given moment.

Conversely, what you can do, among other things, is watch where the market starts to lose steam, and either get out of a position, switch counters, or short the asset. The possibilities of how to read the market and what to do get pretty sophisticated once you start to get comfortable with the OBV. But the two things that you absolutely must keep your eye on is the pending trades and the OBV.

There is also something called the OBV mismatch, and it is a trade of the second order in the sense that you are no longer just looking at the price of things to determine a trade; you are looking at the effect of the activity around it that is measured by the OBV.

If you find that there is a mismatch between two cryptos, then you go to the price that they are trading at and determine if the price of the cryptos are converging or diverging. If you find them converging, then prepare yourself for a sell order. If they are diverging, do the opposite.

Chapter 4:

Trading Indicators

Within the next decade, or less, trading in cryptos is going to be dominated by algorithms and artificial intelligence. There is not much to dispute on that. We have already started to see that equities and bonds have started using Quants (Quantitative Analysts). Quants in traditional markets are similar to the technical traders we talked about earlier in the book when it comes to trading cryptos. They essentially trade on statistical and mathematical strategies.

Don't worry, you don't need to be a mathematician to do any of this. What you do need to do is get started now, so that when the time comes, and you want to remain competitive, you will be able to understand what the technical analysis is and how the program you get into will be able to assist you when trading cryptos. Remember that cryptos, more than anything else, naturally lend themselves to program trading.

There are four market zones that you need to be aware of. The first one is the Japanese time zone, which starts at about 8pm EST and ends at 4pm EST. During this time you get fair volume. Then comes the Middle East Market, which opens at about midnight EST and stretches to 8am EST. This overlaps with the European Market and stretches the active tomes to about 10am EST, by which point the US east coast comes online and kicks up the volume, and that stretches all the way to about 8pm EST due to the west coast.

Even though these are 24-hour, 7-day week markets, there are peak times that you need to be aware of. If you are not using an AI to monitor the volumes, then you can just use these times in your program to assume that these are the times – especially the times when there is an overlap that there will be greater volume and better use of statistical and computational strategies. Increased volume plus increased volatility make trading profitable, and that is a function of peak overlap business hours.

Moving Averages

Whether you get a sophisticated system, or you decide to run the numbers by hand, you need to start your technical education with the simplest and most effective tool that you will find. It is called Moving Averages and you will see them denoted in forms like MA-30, MA-5 and so on. MA of course stands for Moving Average. But the number that follows it represents the period that the average is computed for. So MA-30 represents the moving average of prices over the last 30 periods.

Note that I wrote 'periods' and not days. The reason is that the time-scale is up to you. If you are looking at short-term trades, then the time-scale can be as small as 30 seconds or a minute or even 5 minutes. If your investment horizon is in the long-term, then you would use days. You can even use them in conjunction to understand the longer trend and the short-term fluctuations.

For instance, you can use a 30-day moving average to get a feel for the long-term trend, and that would give you y0ur bias. So, for instance if the trend indicated an up-swing, then you would have a bias that the prices are going up, and that you should favor long (long is the term used to indicate buy positions) positions. If the long-term trend is moving downward, then you should have a bias for short positions (short is the term for selling).

Typically, you would use two long-term trends, let's say an MA-35 and an MA-21 (I find that using Fibonacci numbers gives better results). This timescale is measured in days. That will give you the long-term bias. Then you can have the short-term indicators, like the MA3 and MA8. These are measured in minutes. So, I take the price at the end of a minute, three times consecutively, then add them up and divide it by 3. So, let's say at 9:01am the price is 10. At 9.02am the price is at 10.5, and at 9.03am the price is at 10.8. You would take 9, 10.5, and 10.8 and add them up to get 30.3. Divide that by 3 (since it is three periods) and you will get 10.1. As such, the MA3 is 30.1. You will then plot that line and superimpose that plot on the price chart. What you will find is a smoothed out price movement chart. If you then superimpose the MA8, which is the 8-period average, then you have two similar lines that tend to flow together.

The signal comes when one line crosses the other. When the MA3 is below the MA8, it indicates a falling trend, and when the MA3 is above the MA8 it indicates a rising trend. This is your short-term indicator.

The same happens with your long-term indicator. If the long-term indicator (the one measured in days) shows a longer-term trend, this can form your extended bias. So, if the long-term trend is set to rise, that is your long-bias. Thus, if you have a long-bias that is necessitated by the longer MA, and the short-term trend indicated by the shorter MA, then what you have is a good position to scalp the market in both directions whichever way it goes.

Here is how you do that.

If the long-term MA is a long bias, then you keep your eye on the fact that the market is poised to turn up quickly, and so you start with a footing of a buy position. As soon as the short-term indicator also shows a buy signal, then you jump into the market. The moment the short-term indicator changes to the sell, then you liquidate that position, and enter a new short position. But this second short position needs to be more sensitive. At the first indication of the short-term changing back to the buy, you liquidate that position, reap the profit, and also enter a new buy position. You keep doing this at every opportunity, especially when there is large volume in the market during peak time. This indicator is most effective and accurate when the market is liquid.

This is a good indicator, and in unsophisticated markets is strong enough to be the only indicator that you will need to profit from a market. If you start doing program trades, which you should, then just use the test feature in the app to test the strategy on past price movements and observe the trade signals. I have done this many times while programming the AI version of the trade algorithm and the rapid-fire efficacy – which is to take every trade every time without hesitation. Strict programmatic trading resulted in 81% accuracy of trades and a 27% return in a day. (this was in test mode, not live market). That was the program trade version. In the AI version, we programmed the engine (AI engine) to run millions of simulations until it found the best interval and the most accurate signal. The results were better than expected, and it is one of the reasons I mentioned earlier that crypto trading will be fully programmatic or AI-driven within the next decade. So you might as well get on board now.

Exponential Moving Average

The EMA has a little more efficiency to it in certain markets, especially the BTC-USD rates. It is exactly the same as the MA that we saw above, with the only difference being that there are weights applied to different periods. The rationale behind this is that the number that are close to the present moment in time should count more toward the average than a number that is much further in the past. This calculation has its advantages and works well in BTC-ETH exchange, and a couple of other crypto-crypto rates. It also works better in markets that are less volatile. Less volatile markets tend to result in indicators that are too sensitive, which then results in a higher incidence of false positives.

Here is how you do it:

Use a Fibonacci number again to choose the time horizon. Let's say you take 13 periods. Apply a weight of 1.3 to the most recent number, 1.1 to the number before that, 1 to the number before that, and go all the way back to 0.1 for the first number in the sequence. So, let's say the following sequence is the price of the asset over the last 13 periods:

10,9,10,11,12,11,12,13,12,11,13,14,13

Multiply each number by its weight, like this:

10(0.1),9(0.2),10(0.3),11(0.4),12(0.5),11(0.6),12(0.7),13(0.8),12(0.9),11(1.0),

Then add up all those numbers

1+1.8+3+4.4+6+6.6+8.4+10.4+10.8+11+14.3+16.9 = 94.6

Then divide 94.6 by the sum of the weights, which is 9.1

So 94.6/9.1 = 10.39

You can play around with the weights of the prices to fine tune it to your favorite counter, but you now get the picture. In case you were wondering, yes, you use two horizons—EMA 13 and EMA21—and when they cross over, it indicates a trigger to purchase or sell.

When the faster of the two is above, then it is a buy, and when the slower is above it's a sell indication. You can use this in conjunction with the regular moving average for certain counters. In my experience, it seems to work well with the less volatile pairings like Ethereum vs Ripple, or Ripple vs Monero.

ADX Indicators

The final indicator that I want to introduce you to is the ADX. But before we get into that, I want to impress upon you that the way to make money in crypto trading is not so much about identifying the trends of a price movement. It is really about identifying turning points. You make the most return in accurately picking the point where a turn is made in earnest – that means you are able to look over the false positives. In trades you want to get in at the start of a run and keep scalping the mini moves. That's why a 24-hour market works so well, because the market lends itself to constant data analysis. There are no sudden starts and stops – discontinuities that leave risk to accumulate from the close of one session to the open of the next. I have said this in an earlier part of the book. It is statistically more prudent to liquidate and square your positions at the end of your trading day than to leave open positions unattended – especially when you do not have a program or AI engine running your trades.

The ADX is a line chart that is plotted on the price chart. Typical price charts represent the movement of the price in graphical presentation. Charts give you visual cues which are better to work with manually, and conceptualize strategies for. But programs do not see things in chart presentation, they see it in equations, variables and data. But for you and me, the visual representation works well – like seeing the analog needle of your car's speedometer is more effective than seeing digital numbers.

You don't need to know how to exactly calculate the ADX, because it is not something that is of much use unless it is done in real-time to evaluate a trade, and most programs and web trading portals provide it. Instead of showing you the long and tedious calculations, I think it will be time well spent to describe its efficient use.

With the ADX plotting in real-time at the bottom of the chart and the moving averages superimposed on to the price chart, what you get is one statistic backing up another. The ADX shows you the momentum of the counter or the move. It goes between 0 and 100 and that indicates the percentage of strength. Anything above 80 shows significant momentum in a particular trend, and anything below 30 shows little (or none). When the ADX line breaks 30% you can start to see a momentum build in the price and you can reconfirm this with the overlapping MA. This gives you an assurance of the signals.

If you are thinking that this just sounds like more work for no additional payoff, I couldn't agree with you more. Where this really comes in hand is when you place this as part of a trading program and the program automatically checks the momentum to determine if a trade is viable. So, in the work up to running algorithms to signal your trades, you should get used to using the ADX so that when the time comes you will be able to tweak the parameters to get better results from the trade recommendations.

Chapter 5:

Artificial Intelligence and Algorithms

This is going to be a short chapter because it is only intended to introduce you to AI and programmatic trading. It is my strongest belief that you should get into AI trading, or at the very least programmatic trading, as quickly as possible.

Many traders talk about the art of trading and getting a feel for the market before you actually get into programs and algorithms. But I am in it for the money, and so are you, I assume.

In that case, the thing that you want to invest in, in addition to the T1 line and the Bloomberg Terminal, is a comprehensive trading algorithm and an artificial intelligence platform. They may seem like the same thing, but they are not at this juncture.

The algorithm is one where you can pull various data feeds and tell the program what you want it to do, and it will do exactly what you tell it. If there is a mistake in the program, or the logic in the concept is faulty, you will get suboptimal results and you will have to tweak it yourself over time.

AI on the other hand is self-learning. If something is self-learning that means you get to tell it what output you want, and if that output is wrong, it will continue to chew on the data to arrive at predictions that are accurate.

The way we run our AI is to feed it millions of points of data and run specific instructions that it will then look at and make a prediction, it will then look at the subsequent price data and see if its predictions are correct. If they are, the program learns. If it's wrong, it learns that as well, then changes the parameters until it learns so far ahead that its predictions and strategies become highly effective and accurate. That's what you want. That takes time, as the market is constantly evolving.

Within ten years you will get to the point that you can leave that program to do the trading while you hang out with your pals and take on a new expensive hobby. After all, that's the whole point of AI, and crypto-economics and cryptocurrency trading are ideal markets to run AI.

Conclusion

The idea of this book is to give you an understanding of cryptos, how they work and how they behave in market conditions. It also serves as a launching point for you to get the best trading mindset and the understanding of what you should or shouldn't do to make money in this market. If you are planning to enter small, that's fine, but make sure you have the infrastructure to support your trades. Don't just open a trading account and hit the buy or sell button based on recommendations you find on random websites.

The trading of Cryptocurrencies is in its infancy, and it is the best time to get into it. The convergence of AI and cryptos has made it a huge area of growth and wealth creation. I can't stress this enough, do not waste your time and resources on random accounts and trades. You have to make this a focus and an endeavor. This is serious business and you should bring a serious mindset to the table.

Whether you look at Bitcoin or Altcoins (Altcoins is the term given to all other cryptos that are not Bitcoin) the trading strategies are the same. Their underlying blockchain may differ, but the nature of the exchange and the way to profit from it remains identical.

Within your basket of investment, spend more time looking at Bitcoin and Ethereum, but also have a healthy exposure to the other nine cryptos that we mentioned earlier in the book.

There will be more cryptos entering the market in the next few years, and then after that, you will see a consolidation of several them and the attrition of a large number of tokens and other coins. What you will see is the nature of evolution play out over the next ten years, and you will have a front seat to it if you indeed get into this full-time.

Do not hesitate to invest in the infrastructure and get to know the nature of the market. It will carry the day.

References

In addition to the material that you have read here I think you will find these links useful in your quest of greater knowledge in Cryptocurrencies.

https://cryptocurrencyfacts.com/how-to-trade-cryptocurrency-for-beginners/

https://blockgeeks.com/guides/what-is-cryptocurrency/

https://hackernoon.com/the-ultimate-guide-to-understanding-blockchain-and-cryptocurrencies-f37cf4c0043

https://www.ibm.com/developerworks/cloud/library/cl-blockchain-basics-intro-bluemix-trs/

https://bitcoin.org/en/how-it-works

https://99bitcoins.com/bitcoin-basics/

https://ethereumnoobs.com/topics/ethereum-basics/

https://yourstory.com/2017/12/laymans-guide-to-ethereum/

https://www.fxempire.com/education/article/a-basic-introduction-to-ripple-458661

https://blockonomi.com/monero-guide/

CPSIA information can be obtained
at www.ICGtesting.com
Printed in the USA
BVHW011513301121
622757BV00004B/236